Elephants

Written by Lauri Kubuitsile
Illustrated by Andy Elkerton

Fun elephant facts

Elephants are very, very big! A male elephant is called a bull. A female elephant is called a cow.

An elephant weighs as much as two and a half small cars. That's heavy!

Elephants are as tall as two people!

Elephants have got large ears. They wave their ears, and this cools them.

Amazing Fact

Elephants can sleep when they are standing up.

An elephant's trunk

Elephants have got a long nose, called a trunk. It is very strong. Elephants use their trunks to pull up trees!

But elephants can also use their trunks to pick up small sticks.

Elephants use their trunks to drink. They suck water up and squirt it into their mouths.

An elephant's tusks

Many elephants have got two long teeth, called tusks. Elephants use their tusks for many things.

They dig for water with their tusks.

They take bark off trees with their tusks.

Male elephants use their tusks to fight.

Amazing Fact

An elephant's tusks never stop growing.

What do elephants eat?

Elephants eat plants. They also eat seeds, roots, fruit and tree bark. They can eat cabbages and apples, just like you!

Amazing Fact

Elephants eat for about 16 hours every day!

Two kinds of elephant

There are two kinds of elephant: African elephants and Asian elephants.

an African elephant

an Asian elephant

- African elephants are tall, with big ears.
- Most African elephants have got big tusks.

- Asian elephants are short, with small ears.
- Female (and some male) Asian elephants haven't got tusks.

What kind of elephant am I?

Elephant families

Elephant families are called herds. An elephant herd usually has about 10 to 20 elephants in it, but sometimes there are hundreds! There are cows and young bull elephants in the herd.

When bulls are between 12 and 15 years old, they leave the herd.

Elephants at work

Elephants help people in many different ways.

Elephants can carry heavy things.

Elephants can help to clear land for farming.

Amazing Fact

An elephant can lift about 300 kilograms!

Elephants in danger

There are not many elephants left in the world. Hunters kill elephants for their tusks. They can sell the tusks for a lot of money.

But many people are helping elephants. They are safe from hunters in big game parks. Tourists can visit the parks and see the elephants.

The Elephant's Friend

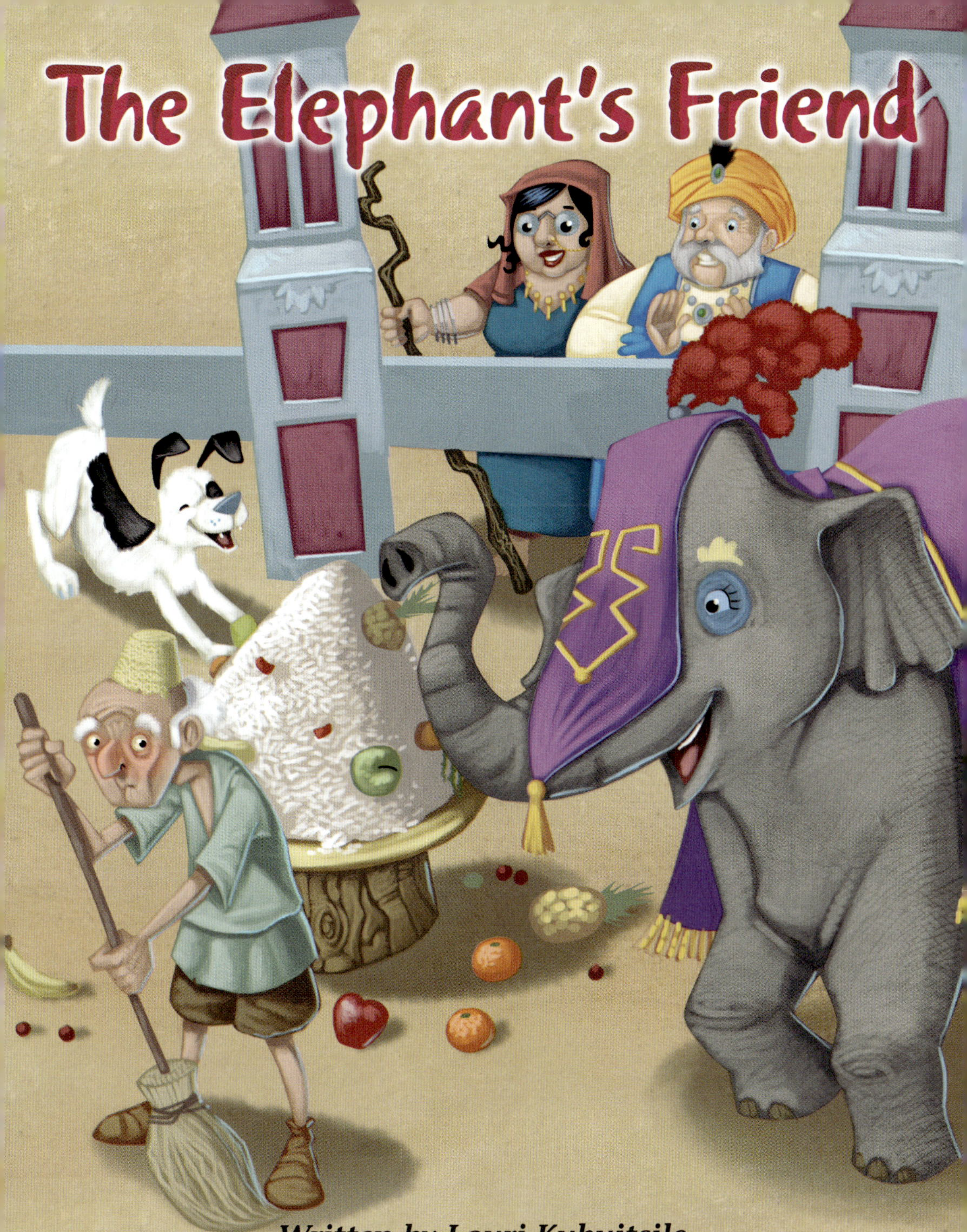

Written by Lauri Kubuitsile
Illustrated by Andy Elkerton

King Daman has got a new elephant in his castle. He brings her to Omar, his elephant keeper.

Omar feeds Ela, then he goes away. He does not see the dog that is hiding nearby.

The dog does not have a home. He is hungry. When Ela drops food on the floor, the dog eats it.

The dog eats with Ela every day. They are good friends now.

One day, Omar sees the dog.

The next day, a man wants to buy Jay. Omar likes Jay, but he needs money.

Ela misses her friend Jay. She is very sad.

The next day, King Daman visits his elephants. When he sees Ela, he is very worried.

King Daman calls Bindah, the wise woman. Can she help?

Bindah visits the elephants.

Bindah sees some paw prints.

Bindah tells King Daman about the thief.

The king asks the people to find the man with the moustache.

The people look for the man. They want the king's gold.

One day, a woman finds the man with the moustache. The king's soldiers bring him to the castle.

King Daman does not believe the man.

The soldiers take the man away to prison, and Omar sees them. Now he is very sorry!

Omar goes to the king. He tells the truth, and King Daman is very angry!

The man with the moustache brings Jay to King Daman. Omar gives the man his money.

The king is worried. What can he do with Omar? He talks to Bindah.

King Daman forgives Omar. Then they take Jay to see Ela.

Ela and Jay are together again. They are very happy!

Activities

1 Complete the sentences with the words *African* or *Asian*.

1 African elephants have got big ears.

2 Female __________ elephants haven't got tusks.

3 Most __________ elephants have got big tusks.

4 __________ elephants are short.

5 __________ elephants are tall.

2 Complete the crossword and find the secret word.

1

2

3

4

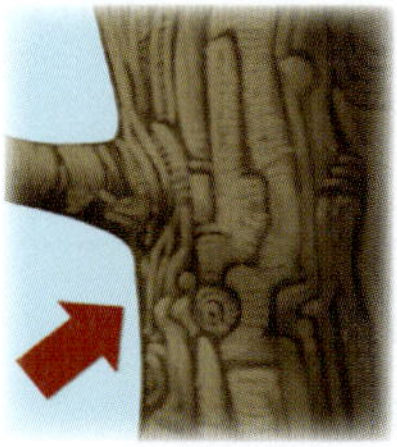

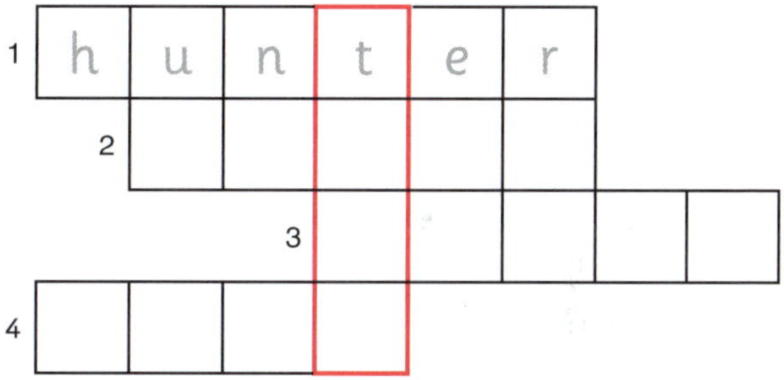

The secret word is: __ __ __ __

3 Match the sentences to the pictures.

1 The elephant is sucking water.

2 The elephant is squirting water.

3 The elephant is pulling up a tree.

4 The elephant is carrying Jay.

a

b

c

d

4 Complete the sentences.

~~ears~~ trunks bark herds Tusks

1 Elephants wave their ___ears___ , and this cools them.
2 __________ are very long teeth.
3 Elephants pull up trees with their __________ .
4 Elephants take __________ off trees.
5 Elephant families are called __________ .

5 Who says it? Match the speech bubbles to the characters.

1 Here is your food, Ela.

2 Her name is Ela. Look after her.

3 Is there a dog here?

4 You are a thief and a liar!

5 I sold the dog to the man with the moustache!

6 He's a good elephant keeper.

a

b

c

6 Circle T (true) or F (false).

1 An elephant weighs the same as two people. T F

2 A male elephant is called a bull. T F

3 Elephants drink water with their tusks. T F

4 Bull elephants leave the herd when they are 12–15 years old. T F

5 Hunters mostly kill elephants for meat. T F

7 Put the story in the correct order. Write the number.

Omar sells Jay to a man with a moustache.	
King Daman asks Bindah to help Ela.	
Jay comes home to Ela.	
Omar tells the truth.	
Ela and Jay become friends.	1
Bindah asks Omar about Ela's friend.	
King Daman tells the people to find the man with the moustache.	
Ela stops eating.	

8 Look at the picture and write the words.

tusks nose ~~teeth~~ ears trunk

1 teeth
2 ________
3 ________
4 ________
5 ________

9 Answer the questions.

1 Has Jay got black and white fur?

Yes, he has.

2 Has King Daman got a moustache?

____

3 Has Omar got glasses?

____

4 Has Bindah got shoes?

____

5 Has Ela got tusks?

____

10 Unscramble the words. Then match them to the pictures.

1 DESE seed

2 FIETH _______________

3 MACEHSTOU _______________

4 NUTHER _______________

a 

b 

c 

d 

Picture Dictionary

male

bull

female

cow

weigh

wave

trunk

pull up

pick up

stick

suck

squirt

tusks

dig

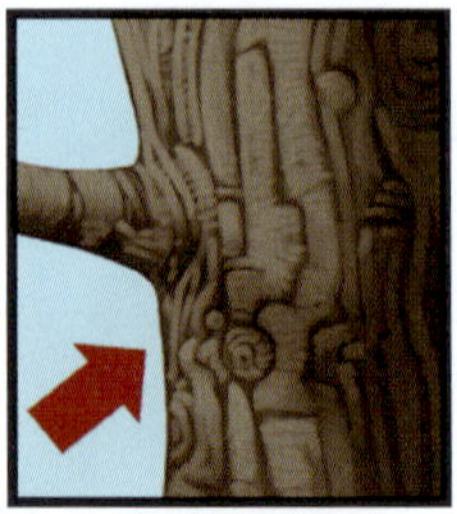
bark

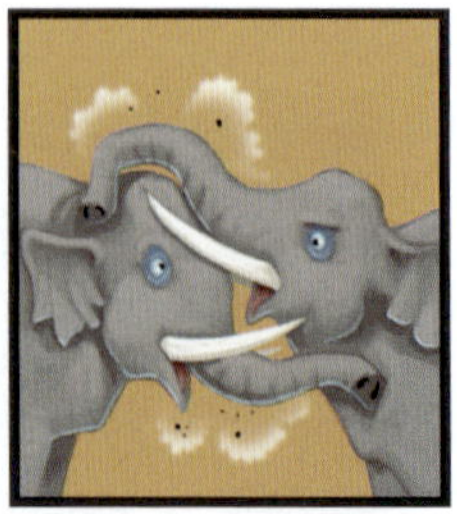
fight

plant

seed

roots

herd

carry

clear land

hunter

king

elephant keeper

hungry

fur

buy

ill

moustache

thief

soldier

Macmillan Education
4 Crinan Street
London N1 9XW
A division of Springer Nature Limited
Companies and representatives throughout the world

ISBN 978-1-3800-3839-5

Written by Lauri Kubuitsile
The author has asserted her right to be identified as the author of this work in accordance with the Copyright, Design and Patents Act 1988.

First published 2013
This edition published 2019

Designed by Carolyn Gibson
Illustrated by Andy Elkerton
Picture research by Victoria Gaunt
Cover photograph by Corbis/DLILLC

The author and publishers would like to thank the following for permission to reproduce their photographic material:
Alamy/bimages p9(bl), Alamy/FLPA p5(tl), Alamy/National Geographic Image Collection p6; **Corbis**/Ocean p8, Corbis/Jami Tarris pp4(br), 5(tr); **FLPA**/Shem Compion p7(l), FLPA/Imagebroker p10(br), FLPA/Ariadne Van Zandbergen pp3(t), 4(t); Getty Images/EyeEm/Patricia De Ley p2, Getty Images/James Hager p5(bl), Getty Images/Stan Osolinski p4(bl); Photodisc p3(b) **Photoshot**/NHPA p7(r); **Rex Features**/EIA p10(tl); **SuperStock**/NaturePL p9(tr).

Printed and bound in Great Britain by Bell and Bain Ltd, Glasgow

2023 2022 2021 2020 2019
10 9 8 7 6 5 4 3 2 1